Good Manners for God's Children

The Scripture quotations in this publication are from The Holy Bible: NEW INTERNATIONAL VERSION. Copyright © 1978 by the New York International Bible Society. Used by permission of Zondervan Bible Publishers.

Copyright © 1984 Concordia Publishing House
3558 S. Jefferson Avenue, St. Louis, MO 63118-3968
Manufactured in the United States of America

1 2 3 4 5 6 7 8 9 10   DB   93 92 91 90 89 88 87 86 85 84

Good Manners for God's Children

By Annetta E. Dellinger

Illustrated by Joe Boddy

CONCORDIA®

Publishing House
St. Louis

"I love you," Jesus said. "You are special to Me. I thought about you long before you were ever born. I knew what you would look like, where you would live, who your friends would be, and even what you would do" (*Psalm 139:1-14*). "You are My children" (*1 John 3:1*).

"That's exciting!" exclaimed Jeremy. "I'm glad we are important to You" (*Isaiah 43:1*).

Maria put her arm around Jesus and said, "We love You more than anything" (*Mark 12:30*).

Jesus smiled. "You all make Me very happy. I'm glad you love Me. I know you will want to love one another, too (*1 John 3:11*). Children, let's not love others only in words or in talk, but let's put our love into action and make it real (*1 John 3:18*). One way to do that is to use good manners."

Jeremy sighed, "You mean I have to be nice to other people?"

Jesus answered: "Yes, you should always be good and loving to others" (*Ephesians 4:32*).

"I remember some things You told us in the Bible about good manners," Chris said. "You want us to love our neighbor as ourself (*Matthew 22:39*) and to treat other people the way we want to be treated (*Luke 6:31*). When I am nice to others, they are nice to me, and everyone feels happy."

"Yes, Chris, you are right. Other people can see that you love Me by the way you act," Jesus replied (*John 13:35*).

"Hi, Jesus! Hi, kids! What are you doing?" Daniel asked as he joined the group.

"We're talking about good manners," Jeremy replied.

"Oh, yes? What's that?" Daniel asked.

"Oh, you know. When Mom calls to get you up in the morning, you're supposed to get right up and not wait to be called a second time," Ryan said.

"Not me!" said Daniel, "I crawl back under the covers and pretend I don't hear her."

"Don't you know that you are supposed to get up with a smile on your face and a cheerful attitude?" Ryan asked. "Say GOOD MORNING to your family and to Jesus."

"My 'good morning' sounds more like a groan than words," said Daniel.

"Well, do you wash your face, comb your hair, and make sure all your clothes are picked up, so your room looks neat and tidy?" asked Ryan.

"You must be kidding! I never hang anything up," said Daniel. "I make my room neat and tidy by leaving things all over the floor!"

"Jesus, I think I know some nice things to do," Maria said." Wash your hands before you eat. Fold your hands and close your eyes during the prayer."

Jesus nodded His head as if to say, "You are right, Maria."

"But I like to peek out of one eye to see if everyone else has their eyes closed," Daniel told her.

"You've got to be kidding, Daniel," Maria said. Then she continued. "Try to eat slowly, chew with your mouth closed, and never talk with your mouth full of food. It looks terrible, and no one can understand what you are saying."

"That is a lot to remember!" Daniel said.

"But that's not all," Maria told him. "You should not play with your food. Don't be a picky eater. Try some of everything."

"Not me!" shouted Daniel. "I eat only the things I like!"

"Daniel," Maria asked, "Do you slurp your soup? You're not supposed to, you know."

"Oh, yes! I love the loud noises I make when I slurp soup!" said Daniel.

"No! No!" Maria said. "Well, . . . do you keep your elbows off the table when you eat?"

"Sometimes," said Daniel.

"Do you tell the cook the food tastes good when you like something?" Maria asked.

"Should I?" asked Daniel.

"Oh, yes. And one more thing," Maria added. "After the meal, say thanks for the food, ask to be excused, and then help clear off the table."

"Who me? Clear off the table!" Daniel said. "I would rather go play."

Jesus put His arm around Daniel and then looked at Maria. "I feel happy when you try to do these things."

Jeremy wanted to tell Daniel about some good habits, too. "If you are sick, take only the medicine your parents give to you. When you cough, yawn, or sneeze, cover your mouth. Throw used tissues in the trash basket."

"Do you mean I am to cover my mouth every time?" Daniel asked.

"Oh, yes. It's not healthy to share germs. Would you want to make your friends sick?" Jeremy asked.

"No, I wouldn't want to do that," Daniel replied.

Jesus asked the children where they should practice doing these things.

Ryan knew. "Home is a good place to begin practicing your manners, but you should practice them everywhere. You could practice closing the doors quietly and walking—not running—when you are inside at home. Then you will remember to do these things when you go away," Ryan said. "And remember to pick up your toys and other things when you are finished with them."

"I don't like to pick up my toys," said Daniel. "After all, I'll probably come back and play with them again."

"Wouldn't you feel terrible if someone fell over your toys and got hurt?" Ryan asked.

"Yes, I probably would," said Daniel.

"And wouldn't you feel awful if you left your toys on a stairstep and someone fell and hurt himself badly?" Ryan continued.

"Oh, that would be terrible! I never thought of someone getting hurt because I was careless," Daniel said.

"Do you know not to play with matches? You could burn yourself or set your home on fire," Jeremy said. "And never, never ask a stranger to come in your home. Let your parents invite people you don't know into your home."

"You mean that I should never, never, never invite strangers into my home?" asked Daniel.

"Right!" replied Jeremy.

"I don't think I'll ever do that, because I wouldn't want someone to hurt me or my family," Daniel answered.

Ryan looked at Daniel, raised his eyebrows, and hesitatingly asked, "Do you ever answer the phone?"

"Of course!" said Daniel. "I pick up the receiver and yell, 'Who is it?' "

"No! No!" Ryan said. "Cheerfully say HELLO. When the person tells you who he wants to speak to, ask WHO IS CALLING, PLEASE, and then say JUST A MINUTE, PLEASE. Lay the receiver down softly and quietly call the person to the phone. If the person is not home say I'M SORRY, BUT HE IS NOT HERE NOW. MAY I TAKE A MESSAGE? Remember to tell your parents who called when they return home."

"I never thought of that before," said Daniel. "I just thought that it was fun to yell into the phone when I answered."

Maria shook her head. Then she looked at Jesus and said, "I am trying hard to not complain when my family askes me to help them do chores or when it is time to take a bath, even when I don't want to."

Jesus held Maria's hand and said, "I am glad you try to be cheerful" (*Proverbs 15:13*).

"Hey, Maria," Daniel laughed, "I love to take a bath. Sometimes my mother tells me she can't find me because I have so many toys in the tub!"

Chris giggled, "One time my parents couldn't find me. I got lost when we were shopping. Now I stay close to them when we're in a crowd. That way I will be safe."

"I know another way to be safe," Jeremy said. "Always sit still and never jump around when riding in the car. Don't stick anything out the window when the car is moving."

"But I can't see out the window when I sit on the seat," Daniel said.

"Yes, I know what you mean! I can't either. But it's important to do this in case there is an accident," Jeremy said. "And remember this, Daniel: Never, never, never ride with a stranger!"

"Okay! Okay! Jeremy. I will never ride with a stranger," said Daniel. "Is that all the good manners I need to remember?"

The boys and girls looked at each other and at Jesus. They all smiled and giggled. Then Maria said, "Do you really want to know some more things?"

"Well. . . ," said Daniel.

"You can really practice good manners at school. For example, try not to giggle when someone gives the wrong answer. Don't copy from someone else's paper. Don't shove in front of others. Try not to brag by saying, 'I'm the best,' or, 'I'm better than you are!' Take turns and play fair by following the rules. When you lose, don't get angry. Tell the winners they did a good job." Maria said.

"But I like to win all the games! And I like to be first in line all the time!" Daniel said as he.

"No, no, Daniel," Maria said, "Don't you think you could try to do these things? You would be surprised how happy you can feel inside when you are kind and thoughtful."

"Wait a minute," Chris said as she smiled at Jesus and put her arm around Him. "When you go to church, sit still and don't squirm. If you need to talk, whisper. If you disturb others, they can't worship God."

"It's hard to sit still and be quiet in church," Daniel said. "My hands want to wave to my friends, and my legs want to make me bounce around."

"I understand," said Chris. "But do you take part in the service? Do you stand up when the people stand, sing when others sing? Do you listen to the pastor when he talks about Jesus?"

"Well . . . not always," said Daniel. "Do you?"

"Sometimes my mother needs to remind me, but I do like to fold my hands and close my eyes during the prayers," said Chris. "Do you?"

"Don't you remember, I like to peek around and see if everyone else has their eyes closed," Daniel replied.

"But I do know that you are not to tear pages in the books, write in them, or run in God's house," Daniel smiled and said.

"Yea! Daniel. You are right! We're proud of you," said Chris and Maria.

"Well, most of the time I don't run in church. However, sometimes my legs forget and then I need to tell them, WALK!" said Daniel.

"Excuse me, Jesus, I know some special words to use no matter where you are," Ryan said. "PLEASE is a word that makes people happy to help you when you need or want something.

"THANK YOU when you are given something and NO THANK YOU when you do not want something.

"I'M SORRY when you want to be forgiven. Instead of talking when other people are talking say EXCUSE ME."

"What were those words again, Ryan?" Daniel asked.

"PLEASE, THANK YOU, NO THANK YOU, I'M SORRY, and EXCUSE ME," Ryan answered.

"I've got it! I guess I've heard them before, and I've even used them once in a while. However, many times I forget to say them," Daniel told Ryan. Then he sat down beside Jesus and began to think.

Jeremy looked at Ryan and then at Jesus. He hung his head and softly said, "Me too. Even though I try to be polite, sometimes I forget. I'm sorry, Jesus" (*Psalm 38:18*).

Jesus held the children close. "Yes, I know you forget. Your sins are forgiven (*1 John 1:9*). I never stop loving you" (*Jeremiah 31:3*).

Dear Dad
I'm Sorry

Jeremy looked down at Daniel and asked, "Do you know now what good manners are?"

Daniel looked at Jeremy and smiled. "Well, I think so."

Daniel smiled at Jesus and then crawled up on His lap. "Jesus, I always thought I had to be nice to people because it pleased my parents."

"Yes, Daniel, you should want to please your parents," Jesus said (*Ephesians 6:1*).

"But now I know the real reason I should use good manners," Daniel said.

"What is the real reason you want to be kind and thoughtful to others?" asked Jesus.

"It's because I love YOU, Jesus!" said Daniel. "YOU make ME feel so happy! You never stop loving me even when I forget to be mannerly. You made me, and I know I'm important to You because You give me everything I have—family, friends, home, food, clothing. YOU take care of me everywhere I go because I am YOUR child. Wow, Jesus, I love YOU too!" Daniel said as he gave Jesus a big hug.

Jesus smiled and held Daniel close to Him.

"You are so good to me," giggled Daniel. "Using good manners will be fun now that I know this makes YOU happy."

"We all love YOU," said the children. "And we want to show everyone how much we love YOU. Thanks for helping us to put love in everything we do and say."

No one has ever seen God; but if we love each other, God lives in us, and his love is made complete in us.

1 John 4:12

SCRIPTURE REFERENCES

Psalm 139:1-14

O Lord, you have searched me and you know me.

You know when I sit and when I rise; you perceive my thoughts from afar. You discern my going out and my lying down; you are familiar with all my ways.

Before a word is on my tongue you know it completely, O Lord. You hem me in—behind and before; you have laid your hand upon me.

Such knowledge is too wonderful for me, too lofty for me to attain.

Where can I go from your Spirit? Where can I flee from your presence? If I go up to the heavens, you are there; if I make my bed in the depths, you are there. If I rise on the wings of the dawn, if I settle on the far side of the sea, even there your hand will guide me, your right hand will hold me fast.

If I say, "Surely the darkness will hide me and the light become night around me," even the darkness will not be dark to you; the night will shine like the day, for darkness is as light to you.

For you created my inmost being; you knit me together in my mother's womb.

I praise you because I am fearfully and wonderfully made; your works are wonderful, I know that full well.

1 John 3:1

How great is the love the Father has lavished on us,
that we should be called children of God.

Isaiah 43:1

I have called you by name; you are mine.

Mark 12:30

Love the Lord your God with all your heart and with all your soul and with all your mind and with all your strength.

1 John 3:11
We should love one another.

1 John 3:18
Dear children, let us not love with words or tongue
but with actions and in truth.

Ephesians 4:32
Be kind and compassionate to one another,
forgiving each other, just as in Christ God forgave you.

Matthew 22:39
Love your neighbor as yourself.

Luke 6:31
Do to others as you would have them do to you.

John 13:35
All men will know that you are my disciples
if you love one another.

Proverbs 15:13
A happy heart makes the face cheerful.

Psalm 38:18
I confess my iniquity; I am troubled by my sin.

1 John 1:9
If we confess our sins, he is faithful and just and will forgive
us our sins and purify us from all unrighteousness.

Jeremiah 31:3
I have loved you with an everlasting love.

Ephesians 6:1
Children, obey your parents in the Lord, for this is right.